Horrible Histories

guilty!

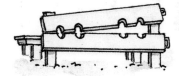

CONTENTS

Watts Books
London • New York • Sydney

LAW AND ORDER

Laws have been written down for at least 4,000 years. The oldest that we know of were written by the Sumerian king, Ur-Nammu, about 2100 BC.

Hammurabi, the king of Babylon from 1792 to 1750 BC, later set down more detailed laws. The Greeks, Jews and Romans added to and improved these laws. Most of our modern laws are based on Roman law or on Anglo-Saxon law.

The Ten Commandments given to Moses by God about 3,000 years ago were laws which told the Jews how they should behave.

The Ten Commandments
Worship no god but me.
Do not make for yourselves images.
Do not use my name for evil purposes.
Observe the Sabbath and keep it holy.
Respect your father and your mother.
Do not commit murder.
Do not commit adultery.
Do not steal.
Do not accuse anyone falsely.
Do not desire another man's house;
    do not desire his wife, his slaves,
    his cattle, his donkeys, or anything
    else that he owns.

In Saxon times, someone who killed another person had to pay a sum of money, called *wergild* (blood money) to the family of his victim.

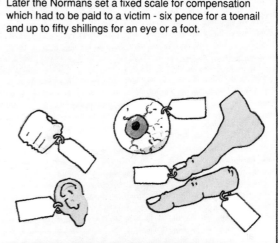

Later the Normans set a fixed scale for compensation which had to be paid to a victim - six pence for a toenail and up to fifty shillings for an eye or a foot.

In ancient China, if somebody accused of a crime was found to be innocent, the accuser was punished instead.

Animals can also be subject to laws. In AD 864, a church court in Germany 'executed' a hive of bees which had stung a man to death.

The law code of the Babylonian King Hammurabi was very severe. If a son hit his father, the son's hand could be chopped off.

In medieval Europe, it was a crime for poor people to wear fancy clothes or jewellery.

The original Hooligans were a family of Irish immigrants who lived in London in the nineteenth century. They were renowned for their violence and lawlessness.

Solon the Law-giver gave a new system of law which was gentler than the previous system to the Greeks of Athens in the sixth century BC.

Solon the Law-giver

International law

The Romans introduced a system of laws called the *Jus Feciale* for all the countries in their Empire. Roman law is the basis for much modern law, including international law.

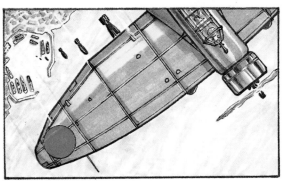

Japan broke international law when it attacked American ships in Pearl Harbor, Hawaii, in 1941, without declaring war. If Japan had declared war on America beforehand, it would have been behaving quite legally.

It was once thought that if a baby's fingernails were cut before its first birthday, it would turn out to be a thief.

STOP THIEF!

Theft is the most common of all crimes and laws against it date back at least 4,000 years. Professional thieves have often formed themselves into gangs. The 'Wild Bunch', led by Butch Cassidy and the Sundance Kid, was a small gang which terrorised the Western Frontier from South Dakota to New Mexico. Some gangs, such as the Mafia, have grown into huge criminal organisations, which profit from many different types of crime.

The last American stagecoach robbery was in 1899. It was carried out by a woman called Pearl Hart.

Billy the Kid (William Bonney 1859-1881) was said to have shot 21 men in the Wild West. He was first jailed for stealing clothes from a Chinese laundry in 1875.

Jesse James once lent a poor widow $800 to repay her debt to a bank. He then robbed the bank and took his money back.

Rogues' Gallery

A bawdy basket was a woman who stole clothes drying on garden hedges.

Anglers stole valuables from open windows using hooks on poles.

Diving belles were female pickpockets in Tudor England.

Footpads stalked their prey on foot. They were muggers.

Highwaymen rode horses and stole from travellers.

When Ned Kelly, the Australian outlaw, was captured in Glenrowan, Australia, in 1880, he was wearing a suit of bullet-proof armour made from melted-down and reshaped ploughshares.

The famous 'Wild Bunch'. Butch Cassidy is seated on the right, and the Sundance Kid is on the left.

The pirate captain Bluebeard used to hang lighted wicks beneath his hat to make himself look frightening.

Organised crime

The Mafia is a network of Sicilian criminal organizations. During the 1890s, Sicilian immigrants introduced it into the USA.

The Japanese Yakuza wear tattoos and execute their victims with swords.

The Triads are Chinese criminal gangs. They prey on Chinese communities throughout the world.

FRAUD AND FORGERY

Some criminals use lies or trickery to steal money or gain power. Forgers manufacture false documents or works of art, which they pass off as genuine. Computer fraud may be carried out by giving false information to computers.

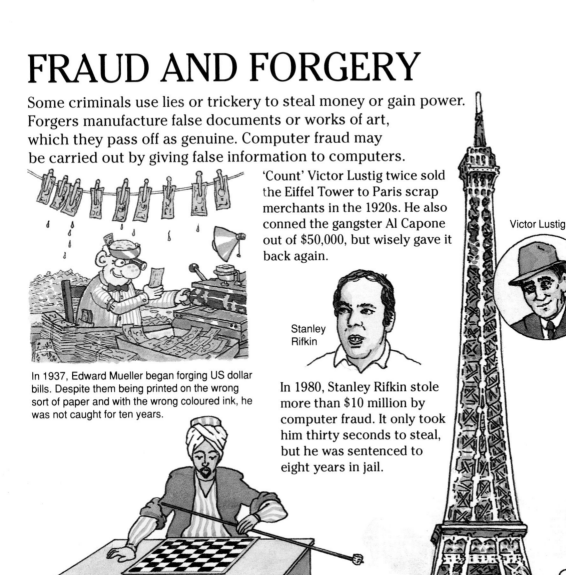

'Count' Victor Lustig twice sold the Eiffel Tower to Paris scrap merchants in the 1920s. He also conned the gangster Al Capone out of $50,000, but wisely gave it back again.

Victor Lustig

Stanley Rifkin

In 1937, Edward Mueller began forging US dollar bills. Despite them being printed on the wrong sort of paper and with the wrong coloured ink, he was not caught for ten years.

In 1980, Stanley Rifkin stole more than $10 million by computer fraud. It only took him thirty seconds to steal, but he was sentenced to eight years in jail.

A machine called The Turk which could play chess made a fortune for its owners between 1769 and 1838 by winning games against expert chess players. It was later discovered that a series of chess-playing dwarfs were hidden inside the machine.

Never give a sucker an even break

The nineteenth century American, Phineas Taylor Barnum, was the world's greatest showman. He exhibited real curiosities and freaks, but many of his attractions were ridiculous frauds. He would exhibit anything as long as his gullible customers paid their entrance fees to see them.

'A cherry-coloured cat' - which was the colour of black cherries!

'A horse with its tail where its head should be'!

'A Fiji Mermaid' - which was made up from a stuffed fish and stuffed monkey.

In many countries, forgers of coins could be put to death. At the time of Elizabeth I in England, if a forger escaped the death penalty, he could be fined, put in the stocks, have his nostrils slit and have his ears lopped off.

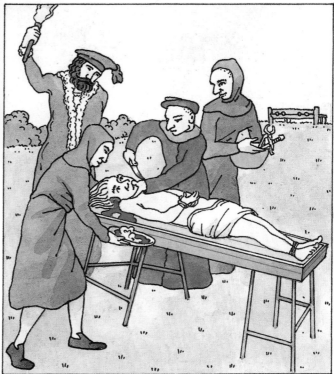

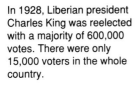

In 1928, Liberian president Charles King was reelected with a majority of 600,000 votes. There were only 15,000 voters in the whole country.

Hans van Meegeren is known as the greatest art forger of all time. His brilliant fakes earned him a fortune, and now, even if they are discovered to be fakes, they are still valuable because he is so famous.

President Ferdinand Marcos of the Philippines diverted $10 billion belonging to his people to his own foreign bank accounts between 1965 and 1988.

As a young man, Michelangelo sold new works of art as antiques. He buried new statues in soil to stain them and make them look old.

MURDER MOST FOUL

It may seem odd, but according to the law in most countries, deliberately killing someone isn't necessarily illegal. For example, during a war, soldiers may kill enemy soldiers without breaking the law. But deliberately killing someone without a legal reason to do so is called MURDER.
Some murders are worse than others.

There was a real Count Dracula - Vlad Dracul who ruled the small country of Wallachia from 1456 to 1476. He didn't suck blood, but he liked to watch his victims being impaled on spikes while he dined. He was known as 'Vlad the Impaler'.

Cannibalism

In 1928, New Yorker Albert Fish killed 10 year old Grace Budd. He cooked and ate parts of her body with carrots and onions. At his trial he said that he was fond of children.

German Fritz Haarmann killed 50 young men between 1919 and 1924 by biting through their throats. He sold the bodies on the black market as beef or pork.

Between 1866 and 1900, twenty thousand American men died from illegal gunshot wounds. The famous Boot Hill Cemetery was so called because most of its occupants had died with their boots on. Many died in street gunfights.

In 1611, Countess Erzsébet of Hungary was tried for the torture and murder of 610 people. She bathed in her victims' blood in order to preserve her beauty.

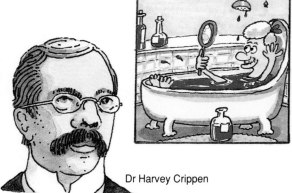

Dr Harvey Crippen

In 1910, Dr Harvey Crippen murdered his wife. His crime was discovered when police found pieces of her flesh buried in Crippen's cellar. Crippen was captured on board a ship bound for Canada, with his mistress who was disguised as a schoolboy. The ship's Captain recognised him and radioed his whereabouts to the London police - the first time radio had been used to capture a criminal. Crippen was arrested as he landed in America. He was later hanged.

Gilles de Rais was accused of the torture and murder of 300 children in France between 1432 and 1440. He was a keen alchemist and needed the blood for his attempts to turn iron into gold.

Tamerlane the Great was a Mongol warlord who built pyramids of the heads of his enemies. He is said to have killed anyone who told him a joke he'd heard before.

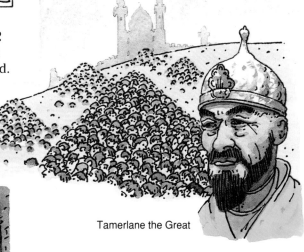

Tamerlane the Great

In London in 1888, at least seven women were brutally murdered by the same person. A letter in red ink boasting about the murders and signed 'Jack the Ripper' was sent to a London newspaper. Jack was never caught, and there have been many different theories about his identity - he was a famous doctor, or he was related to Queen Victoria, or he was even a woman - Jill the Ripper!

ASSASSINATIONS

The murder of important political or religious leaders is called assassination. Political assassinations can lead to riots and even wars where thousands of people may be killed or injured.

In 1914, Archduke Ferdinand of Austria was assassinated by a group of Serbian nationalists called the Black Hand Gang. His assassination was the spark that started the First World War and led to a further 20 million deaths.

Four United States presidents have been assassinated.

Abraham Lincoln was shot whilst watching a play at a Washington theatre by John Wilkes Booth on 14 April 1865. Booth broke his shin when he jumped on to the stage to escape. He went on the run for twelve days and was then captured in Virginia and shot dead.

James Garfield was shot whilst walking to a train by Charles J. Guiteau on 2 July 1881. He died of his wounds on 19 September. Guiteau was hanged a year later.

William McKinley was shot by Leon Czolgosz on 6 September 1901. He died eight days later. Czolgosz was beaten by soldiers and then arrested. A few weeks later, he went to the electric chair.

John Fitzgerald Kennedy was shot in the head by Lee Harvey Oswald on 20 November 1963 from a school book depository. Oswald was later shot and killed whilst on live television.

Roman Emperor Julius Caesar was stabbed more than twenty times by a group of his former colleagues on 15 March 44 BC.

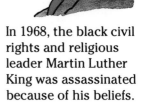

In 1968, the black civil rights and religious leader Martin Luther King was assassinated because of his beliefs.

Roman orator and statesman Cicero wanted a return to a Republican Rome but was opposed by a Roman senator called Mark Anthony. Cicero was assassinated in 43 BC. Mark Anthony's wife stuck pins in his tongue because she had been jealous of his powers of oratory.

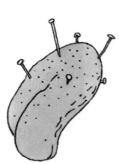

The French revolutionary and leading member of the Jacobin party Jean-Paul Marat was assassinated in his bath by a girl called Charlotte Corday in 1793. She was a supporter of the Girondin party, which opposed the violent Jacobin policies.

Mahatma Gandhi helped end British Rule in India but was assassinated at a garden party by one of his countrymen in 1948.

Most of the Russian royal family was slaughtered by the Communist revolutionaries in 1918 and buried in a secret grave. This grave was later discovered, and in 1993 the bodies were identified as the Russian royal family from traces of DNA in the bones.

Infamous names

The Hashishin were eleventh century Persian religious fanatics who murdered after taking the drug hashish. The word 'assassin' comes from their name.

'Mafia' comes from the Italian word for scrubland. Sicilian outlaws used to live in the 'mafia' hill country.

'Hatchet men' were nineteenth century Chinese gangsters called the Tongs who killed their victims with hatchets.

The word 'thug' comes from 'Thuggee' a Hindu sect (c.1500-1830) which worshipped Kali the goddess of destruction. Members of the sect strangled and robbed up to two million travellers.

GOTCHA!

In the past, ordinary citizens often had responsibility for law enforcement. For instance, in ninth century England, the law said that people must join in any 'hue and cry' and chase suspected criminals. If necessary, soldiers were used to back them up. But soldiers are trained to fight wars and they can be too rough for law enforcement work. So modern societies have developed special law enforcement agencies called police forces.

Wyatt Earp is perhaps the most famous of the Wild West Sheriffs. He was sheriff in the town of Wichita, Texas. In fact, he was not much better than his fellow townsmen. After two years as sheriff he was arrested, fined and fired for disturbing the peace!

The first constables were men who had responsibility for looking after the horses of the Roman Emperors.

The Russian KGB was formed in 1954. For many years it was the largest secret police and spying organisation in the world. At one time it controlled 300,000 border guards as well as a much larger number of other agents.

Gotcha! firsts

Catching criminals by studying their handwriting was first practised by the Romans in AD 500.

The Pinkertons detective agency was set up in the USA in 1850. They were the first to use 'mug-shot' wanted posters.

The first police car was used in Ohio in 1899.

The first lie detector was introduced in the USA in 1921.

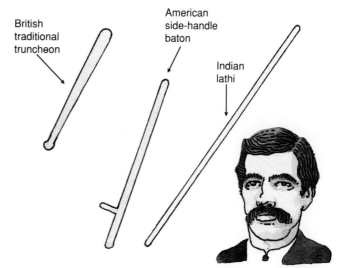

British traditional truncheon

American side-handle baton

Indian lathi

Marshall Tom Smith tried to keep the peace in the lawless Kansas cow-town of Abilene with just his fists. He lasted only five months before being shot dead in November 1870.

The first uniformed English police were the Bow Street Runners founded by the magistrate and writer Henry Fielding between 1748 and 1753. They were paid rewards for catching criminals. In 1829 they were replaced by the modern police force. The new policemen were called 'peelers' or 'bobbies' after their founder Sir Robert Peel.

The 'Mounties', or Royal Canadian Mounted Police, often tracked criminals for weeks through the huge forests of North West Canada. Their motto is 'The Mounties always get their man'.

Kangaroo courts (illegal trials) were common in the Wild West. The name comes from the way the judges 'jumped' to conclusions. Such trials often ended in a lynching (an illegal hanging).

ON TRIAL

When someone is accused of a crime a trial is held to find out if they are guilty or innocent and to decide on a punishment. In many early societies cases were 'tried' by kings, lords or priests. Ordinary people appeared before them to ask them to settle disputes or punish wrongdoers. Nowadays magistrates try petty crimes. More serious crimes are tried by judges or other such experts. In the USA and Britain, serious crimes are tried in front of a judge and a jury. Trial by jury was first developed in ancient Greece. A jury is a group of ordinary citizens selected at random. Most countries also have some sort of supreme court which can alter the decisions of lesser courts. In the USA this is called the Supreme Court. In Britain it is the House of Lords.

During the seventeenth century in England, some men wore straws stuck in their shoe-buckles and were known as 'straw men'. This was to advertise their services, for a fee, as friendly witnesses.

In the Middle Ages, people who could read were treated as priests and received lesser sentences than ordinary citizens. In 1598, playwright Ben Jonson killed a man in a duel. Instead of being hanged he was merely given a small brand on his left thumb!

Judge Roy Bean (1825-1904) was a saloon-keeper and a Justice of the Peace in rough, tough West Texas. He was judge, jury and executioner combined, and had eccentric ideas about the law. He once fined a corpse $40 for carrying a concealed weapon!

The Romans divided citizens into two classes: *honestiores* and *humiliores*. *Honestiores* were rich and were treated gently by the law. *Humiliores* were poor and received harsher punishments. In most countries nowadays, all people are considered equal in the eyes of the law.

A jury may make a wrong decision on purpose because its members have been bribed or threatened. Greek courts had juries of 200 men to make it hard to corrupt them.

Trial by ordeal was common in the Middle Ages. In this type of trial it was assumed that God would show who was innocent and who was guilty.

Trial by combat
Accused and accuser would fight a trial by combat, using swords, knives or lances. The winner was declared innocent.

Trial by fire
The accused had to walk over red-hot ploughshares and pick up a hot iron bar. The hands and feet were wrapped up and examined three days later. If a blister larger than a walnut was found then the prisoner was guilty.

Trial by cheese
Priests were tried by fellow priests. Suspects were given a piece of cheese to eat. If they couldn't swallow it, they were considered guilty.

Trial by water
During the early Middle Ages the accused (often a witch) would be given holy water to drink and then tied up and thrown into a river. If they floated they were guilty and were executed. If they sank they were considered innocent, but they drowned anyway.

PRISON

Prisons have existed for at least 5,000 years. At first they were mainly used to hold hostages or prisoners awaiting trial. After trial, convicted prisoners suffered a variety of other often painful punishments.

During the eighteenth century, some European countries began to send convicts to prison colonies abroad as an alternative, and to save space in their own prisons. This was called transportation. At the same time prison reformers began to protest against executions and other harsh punishments. By 1800, new types of prison were being built. Inmates were treated better than before and loss of freedom became the main punishment. Inmates were encouraged to feel sorry, or penitent, about doing wrong. American prisons even became known as 'penitentiaries'.

Nick names

Criminals have invented many words for prison over the years.

Big house
Can
Chokey
Clanger
Clink
Cooler
Coop
Inside
Jug
Nick
Pen
Pokey
Quod
Slammer
Stir
Tronk

Old ships which were no longer seaworthy, called hulks, were often used as prisons. Many of the prisoners were waiting to be transported.

Between 1791 and 1853, about 45,000 Irish convicts were transported to Australia, as well as many thousands from England, Scotland and Wales.

Until recently, convicts wore special clothes which were easy to spot if they escaped.

American convicts wore striped suits. British prison uniforms were covered in arrow symbols.

Prisoners in America used to be chained together in 'chain-gangs' then taken out to do hard labour such as repairing roads or breaking rocks.

In nineteenth century Russia, convicts were often exiled to Siberia. They were forced to walk there whilst chained hand and foot. The 3,000 mile walk took two years and many died on the way.

From Roman times to the fourteenth century, some criminals were made to row the oars on Mediterranean ships called galleys. They were permanently chained to their oars for years at a time.

Typhus was once known as 'Jail Fever'. The disease is carried by small creatures such as lice or mites which could move easily from one prisoner to another in overcrowded conditions.

Medieval dungeons were often just small, dark holes down a cellar. Some were called 'oubliettes' from the French word *oublier* - to forget. Prisoners were just thrown in and forgotten. The feet of many prisoners rotted away from standing chained up in pools of filthy water.

Treadmill pumps had to be constantly worked by prisoners to keep some of the hulks afloat. Because of the sweat-sores a treadmill caused, it was called a 'Cockchafer'.

Treadmills were also used in ordinary prisons as a punishment.

ESCAPE

It is illegal for convicts or prisoners awaiting trial to escape or try to escape. Even so, many attempt it because of their strong desire for freedom. Escaping is often considered worse than many of the crimes for which a prisoner may have been convicted. This means that a recaptured convict may have several years added to a sentence, or even face death.

Escaper's tool kit - file to file through bars, spade for tunnelling, knotted sheets to act as a rope, bolster to look like sleeping prisoner, hand made clothes, false passport, lock pick, wig for disguise.

Prisons are often built on islands because this makes escape doubly difficult. Alcatraz island in San Francisco Bay was a grim maximum security prison from 1934 to 1962. Twenty-three attempted to escape, but all were killed or recaptured except for five, who were presumed drowned. Alcatraz is now a museum.

Napoleon on the ship *Bellerophon*, bound for Saint Helena as a prisoner of war.

The defeated French Emperor Napoleon Bonaparte escaped from the Mediterranean island of Elba in 1815. He raised an army and marched to Paris. After his defeat at the battle of Waterloo he was exiled to the remote Atlantic island of Saint Helena. There was no escape from this tiny island. He died there in 1821.

In 1880, Billy the Kid escaped from Fort Sumner County Jail even though he was handcuffed and had his legs shackled.

Devil's Island was a famous French penal colony off the coast of South America. One prisoner, named Gerardin, faked the symptoms of leprosy by cutting off his fingers. He was removed to a nearby leper colony island and then he escaped to Brazil.

Unfortunately, it was then found that he really did have leprosy. The Brazilian authorities built him a small prison of his own.

The Tower of London was reserved for the king's enemies. The twelfth century Bishop of Durham, Ranulf Flambard, was the first political prisoner to be imprisoned in the tower. He was also the first to escape after arranging for a rope to be smuggled into the tower inside a wine cask.

Prisoners have often been freed during popular uprisings. The Bastille State Prison in Paris was stormed by an enraged mob of peasants in 1789. Though only seven prisoners were released, this symbolic act helped start the French Revolution.

In 1919, the Irish freedom fighter Eamon de Valera escaped from Lincoln Jail using keys smuggled into the jail hidden inside Christmas cakes. He fled to the USA, later returning to Ireland to become Prime Minister, and then President.

CHAMBER OF HORRORS

'Torture' comes from a Latin word meaning 'to twist'. It was once standard practice and was used to extract confessions. A skilful torturer knew how to keep his victim alive for as long as possible while inflicting the maximum amount of pain. Torture was made illegal in England in 1640 and is now forbidden under international law, although several regimes still make use of it.

A chained prisoner on trial in nineteenth century China

Ancient Chinese water tortures
There were many different tortures involving water.

The victim was tied down underneath a steady drip of water on his forehead which drove him insane.

Bamboo shoots were fed to a victim who was then forced to drink. Over the next few days, the shoots would grow through the stomach and emerge from the skin.

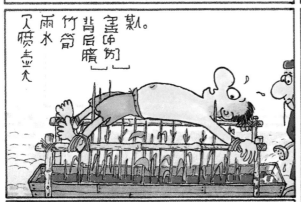

The victim would be tied down over a bed of bamboo shoots. The shoots were watered and would grow up through the victim.

Water would be pumped down the victim's throat until his stomach burst.

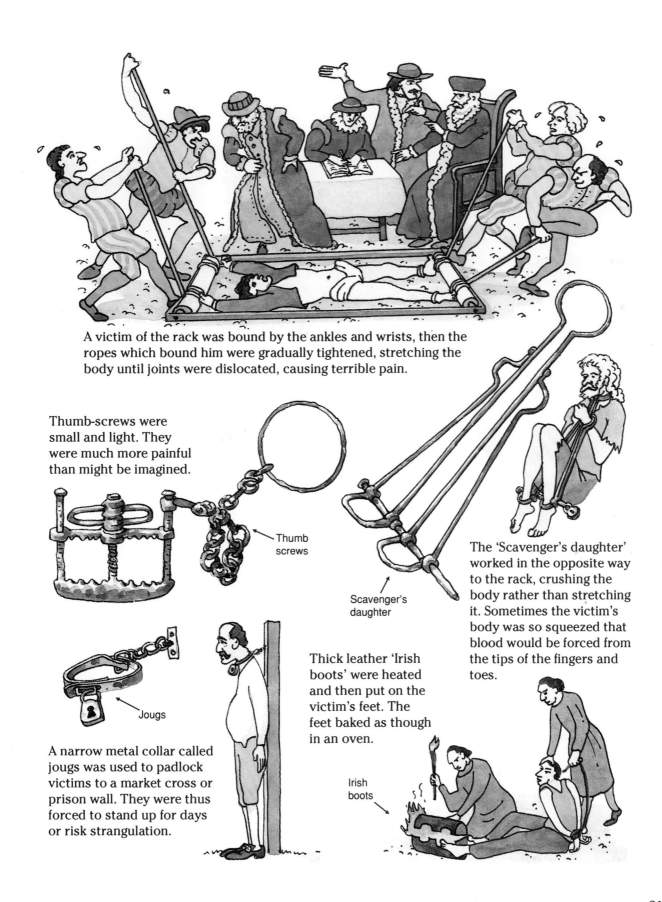

A victim of the rack was bound by the ankles and wrists, then the ropes which bound him were gradually tightened, stretching the body until joints were dislocated, causing terrible pain.

Thumb-screws were small and light. They were much more painful than might be imagined.

Thumb screws

The 'Scavenger's daughter' worked in the opposite way to the rack, crushing the body rather than stretching it. Sometimes the victim's body was so squeezed that blood would be forced from the tips of the fingers and toes.

Scavenger's daughter

Jougs

A narrow metal collar called jougs was used to padlock victims to a market cross or prison wall. They were thus forced to stand up for days or risk strangulation.

Thick leather 'Irish boots' were heated and then put on the victim's feet. The feet baked as though in an oven.

Irish boots

Branding with a hot iron was a common punishment, or ownership mark. Foreheads, cheeks and fingers were the most usual places to be branded.

H = Harlot or Heretic
D = Drunkard
S = Slave
M = Murderer
T = Thief

PUBLIC PUNISHMENTS

In the past many punishments involved public humiliation. This demonstrated the power of the law to the people who passed by, as well as being very unpleasant for the wrongdoer. These sorts of punishment were considered very important in medieval Europe. An English town of the period would not be allowed to hold a market if it did not maintain a pillory. Even small villages might have a ducking stool and a whipping post.

Ducking stools were chairs on the end of a long pole. Victims such as cheating tradesmen, harlots and witches were tied to the chair and lowered into a pond or river until they nearly drowned.

Scold's bridle

Nagging wives were sometimes made to wear a 'scold's bridle' to hold their tongues.

Drunkard's cloak

Drunkards in New England, USA, were forced to wear a 'drunkard's cloak'. This was a barrel with holes cut out for arms, legs and head. It was meant to make them look silly.

People fixed by the hands and head to a pillory had dead rats, rotten eggs or other rubbish thrown at them.

The stocks were less harmful than the pillory - people's hands were free to protect their faces from the rubbish which was thrown at them.

Stocks

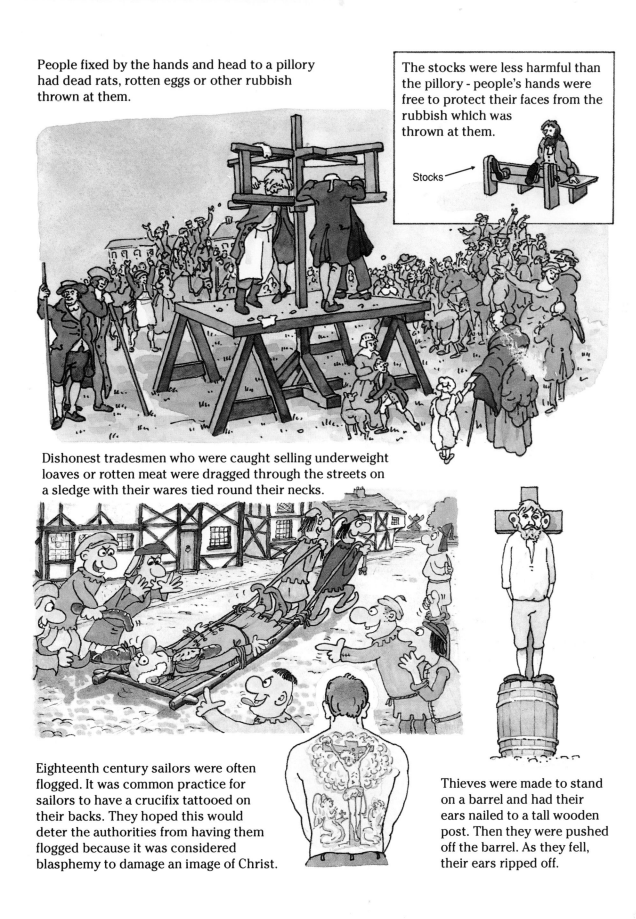

Dishonest tradesmen who were caught selling underweight loaves or rotten meat were dragged through the streets on a sledge with their wares tied round their necks.

Eighteenth century sailors were often flogged. It was common practice for sailors to have a crucifix tattooed on their backs. They hoped this would deter the authorities from having them flogged because it was considered blasphemy to damage an image of Christ.

Thieves were made to stand on a barrel and had their ears nailed to a tall wooden post. Then they were pushed off the barrel. As they fell, their ears ripped off.

WITCHES AND HERETICS

Most primitive cultures have a fear of bad magic. This fear lingered in Europe and America into the recent past and resulted in the persecution of people, especially old women, who were thought to be witches. Witches were often burned at the stake, as were heretics. Heretics were people who questioned orthodox versions of Christianity. Some medieval heretics were hacked to pieces with an axe.

The Spanish Inquisition persecuted Moslems, Jews and Protestants. Thousands of people were burned to death after being convicted of religious crimes and then sentenced at a public ceremony called an *Auto da fé*, or 'Act of Faith'. Victims of burning were often strangled as an act of mercy before the flames consumed them.

The Iron Maiden was used for executions by church officials in medieval Germany. The spikes on the inside of the lid pierced the victim when the lid was closed. The spikes were sometimes arranged so that two of them pierced the victim's eyes.

Iroquois Native Americans executed witches by ripping off their skin and tying them to anthills.

Pincers

In 1589, Frenchman Peter Stube was convicted of being a werewolf. His skin was torn off with red-hot pincers as a punishment.

In medieval Germany, blasphemers might have their tongues ripped out with red-hot pincers.

Women convicted of crimes for which a man might be beheaded were often burnt to death instead. This was because burning was thought to be a more decent way for women to die as it did not involve any cutting of their bodies.

In Salem, Massachusetts, in 1692, two girls aged nine and eleven made accusations of witchcraft. The idea caught on and soon a number of girls had accused more than three hundred people of witchcraft. Twenty of their victims were executed. One of them, Giles Cory, was pressed to death with heavy weights. He was eighty years old.

In 1471, a Swiss cockerel was found guilty of laying an egg 'in defiance of natural law'. It was burnt at the stake as a devil.

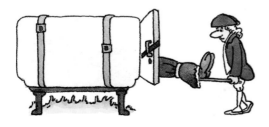

From 1651 to 1660, at least 2,000 women were burnt as witches in Silesia in what is now Poland. They were roasted in huge ovens.

OFF WITH THEIR HEADS!

The execution of wrongdoers is called capital punishment, from the Latin word *caput* meaning 'head'. In the past, decapitation, or death by removal of the head, was considered the most dignified way to die, and was often reserved for the nobility. Common people were more likely to be hanged.

When the guillotine was introduced by M. Guillotin in 1792, decapitation became very efficient. The guillotine was a heavy blade, raised between two poles and set at an angle, which fell on the victim's neck when released. Thousands of French aristocrats were executed with this device during the French Revolution.

The Sansons were a family of French executioners. Charles-Henri Sanson worked for the French revolutionaries. He decapitated over 4,000 people during his career. He sometimes sold their fat as a remedy for rheumatism.

Old ladies called *tricoteuses*, which is French for knitters, sat by the guillotine during the French Revolution. They knitted to pass the time between executions.

FAT

The principal of the guillotine has been known for two thousand years. The Chinese fitted a blade to a swinging tree trunk.

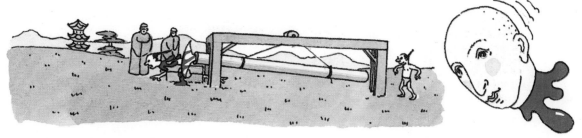

Blood from a decapitated body may jet several feet into the air.

When Mary Queen of Scots was executed, her wig fell from her head. The head rolled on the floor like a ball.

In Germany, decapitation with a sword was a privilege reserved for aristocrats. There, and in some other countries, people who were to be executed by the sword knelt upright. Skilled executioners would slice off the head with one blow.

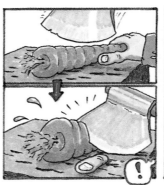

Executioner Jack Ketch was notorious for his cruelty and inefficiency. He took five blows of the axe to execute the Duke of Monmouth. The head was then sewed back on so that Monmouth's portrait could be painted.

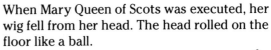

Block   v   Guillotine

An axe-man had to have a perfect aim to be able to decapitate with a single blow. The victim had to be held in exactly the right position.

The guillotine held the victim's neck securely as the blade flashed through it. This helped to give a neat cut every time.

SENTENCED TO DEATH

Throughout history there have been many forms of execution apart from decapitation. In the past many types of execution were meant to be horribly unpleasant.

The Romans favoured crucifixion as a means of execution. Criminals were normally tied to the cross and not nailed to it. Nailing was an extra-painful method. The victims' legs were often broken as an act of mercy to speed death. After the slave revolt led by Spartacus in 72 BC, the Appian Way was lined with 6,000 crucifixes.

The Moors executed Christians by throwing them into snake pits.

The Anglo-Saxons executed traitors by shooting arrows into them.

The Aztecs roasted prisoners alive over fires of chilli peppers.

The Inuit left prisoners tied up on the ice to be killed by polar bears or the cold.

In ancient Egypt criminals were thrown to the sacred Nile crocodiles.

Hanging was a popular entertainment. In 1807, 40,000 people crammed into a London square to watch the double hanging of two criminals called Holloway and Haggerty. Many of the spectators were trampled to death.

Pirates were often executed by being hung by their hands with their toes touching the low water mark of the tide. As the tide rose they slowly drowned.

Saint Katherine of Alexandria was sentenced to be broken on the wheel. This involved tying her to a round frame and then breaking her limbs. The wheel was said to have been shattered by an angel and she was beheaded instead. The firework called a Katherine wheel is named after her.

The Chinese practised a form of execution called 'Death by a Thousand Cuts'. The victim was killed as slowly as possible by a myriad small cuts all over his body.

Hanging, drawing and quartering was a punishment reserved for English traitors. They were first pulled through the town on a wooden frame behind a horse. Then they were hung until half dead. After that they were taken down and their intestines were pulled out before their eyes. This treatment finally killed them. Their arms, legs and head were then chopped up and sent to be displayed in the four corners of the kingdom.

THE FUTURE

Most of the punishments described in this book have been abolished. But crimes are still committed and criminals are still punished. In the future new technologies may make our lives more comfortable, but they will not stop crime. Advances in technology will lead to new types of crime and new forms of control and punishment for those who break the law.

Semi-automatic police such as Robocop or Judge Dredd are popular fantasies, but advances in bio-cybernetics may make such creations possible.

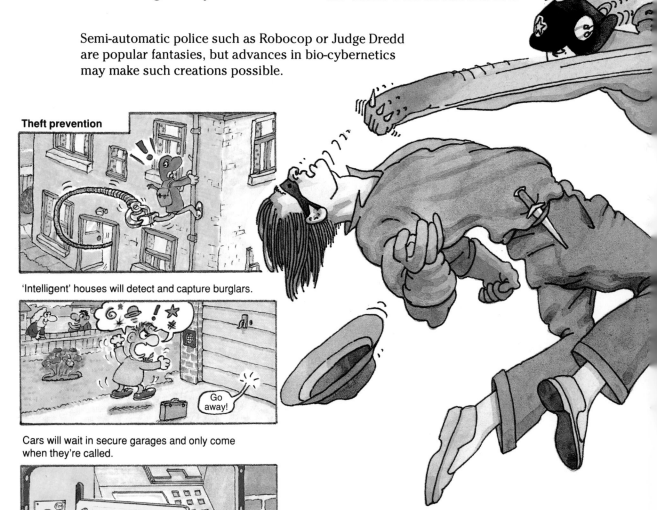

Theft prevention

'Intelligent' houses will detect and capture burglars.

Go away!

Cars will wait in secure garages and only come when they're called.

STREET KRED

Voice-activated credit cards will make fraud more difficult.

Electronic tagging of criminals so their movements can be checked has already been introduced experimentally in California.

Computers will soon be able to store information on the genetic codes of entire populations. Every individual except identical twins has a unique code. It will be easy to identify who has left any small flakes of skin or drops of body fluids such as blood at the scene of a crime.

There are more laws now than ever before. If the number of laws were reduced there would be fewer crimes to commit!

Ordinary citizens may form vigilante groups such as the New York Guardian Angels if crime levels continue to rise.

Perhaps the best solution to crime in the future will have nothing to do with technology. If people live in small communities where they know their neighbours, crime becomes much more unlikely.

INDEX

First published in 1994 by
Watts Books
96 Leonard Street
London EC2A 4RH

Paperback edition 1994

10 9 8 7 6 5 4 3 2 1

Franklin Watts Australia
14 Mars Road
Lane Cove
NSW 2060

© 1993 Lazy Summer Books Ltd
Illustrated by Lazy Summer Books Ltd

UK ISBN 0 7496 1185 5 (hardback)
UK ISBN 0 7496 1597 4 (paperback)

A CIP catalogue record for this book is
available from the British Library
Dewey Decimal Classification: 364

Printed in Belgium